The Oratorio Anthology

Alto/Mezzo-Soprano

Compiled and Edited by Richard Walters

Assistant Editors: Elaine Schmidt, Laura Ward
Repertoire Consultant: Kathleen Sonnentag
Historical Consultant: Virginia Saya

On the cover: André Derain, French, *The Last Supper*, oil on canvas, 1911, 226.7 x 288.3 cm, Gift of Mrs. Frank R. Lillie, 1946.339. © 1993, The Art Institute of Chicago, All Rights Reserved.

ISBN 0-7935-2506-3

HAL•LEONARD
CORPORATION

7777 W. Bluemound Rd. P.O. Box 13819 Milwaukee, WI 53213

Contents

Notes and Translations

Johann Sebastian Bach
1685-1750

MASS IN B MINOR
composed 1724-1740s
text is the traditional Latin Mass from the Roman Catholic liturgy

Not initially conceived as a unity, the different sections of what would eventually be the Mass in B minor were composed over a period of perhaps as much as 25 years. The Sanctus was composed in 1724 and first performed on Christmas Day in that year at Thomaskirche, Leipzig. The Kyrie and Gloria sections, comprising what was then known as the Missa in Lutheran terminology, were composed and first performed in 1733, probably in Dresden. At some later point Bach composed the remaining sections with the result of a complete traditional mass. The sources are unclear, and there is disagreement about the dates of composition for the Credo, Osanna, Benedictus, Agnus Dei, and Dona nobis pacem. Among the new composition there was significant borrowing of music from earlier works. Bach's work to complete the mass was probably done in the 1740s, with theories that put it as late as 1748 or 1749, which would make the Mass in B minor perhaps the composer's last major composition. (*The Art of the Fugue* was most likely principally composed early in the decade.) Earlier historical theories stated that these remaining sections were composed at different times, primarily in the 1730s, and that Bach assembled the mass into a whole near the end of his life. The first performance of the complete work was in 1859 in Leipzig.

Qui sedes ad dextram Patris

"Qui sedes ad dextram Patris" is from the Gloria section of the mass, composed in 1733.

Qui sedes ad dextram Patris,	*Who sits on the right hand of the Father,*
miserere nobis!	*have mercy upon us!*

Agnus Dei

Music for the "Agnus Dei" is taken from church cantata no. 11, the "Ascension Oratorio," composed in 1735.

Agnus Dei	*Lamb of God*
qui tollis peccata mundi,	*who takes away the sins of the world,*
miserere nobis.	*have mercy upon us.*

PASSIO SECUNDUM JOANNEM
(Johannes-Passion/St. John Passion)
BWV 245
1724
libretto based primarily on *Der für die Sünden der Welt gemarterte und sterbende Jesus* (Jesus tortured and dying for the sins of the world) by Barthold Heinrich Brockes (1712), with some additional free texts from a 1704 Passion libretto by Christian Heinrich Postel (free text refers to poetry that is not an adaptation or paraphrase of Scripture), with adaptations and additional material by the composer

Composed in 1723, the Passion was first performed on Good Friday, April 7, 1724 at Thomaskirche, Leipzig. The piece was revised, with additions, deletions and substitutions, for performances in 1725, but basically restored to the original version for performances in c1730 and 1740. A Passion is a musical setting of Jesus' sufferings and death as related by one of the four Gospel writers. Brockes' libretto, cited above, was the most often set of Passion librettos by composers in the 18th century.

Dates throughout are for first performances unless otherwise noted. The bracketed aria titles are those used when performing the singing English translation found in the musical score. The notes in this section are by the editor.

Von den Stricken meiner Sünden *[From the shackles of my transgressions]*

From Part I (no. 11), scored for oboes and continuo. This is a free text from Brockes' libretto.

Von den Stricken meiner Sünden mich zu entbinden, wird mein Heil gebunden. Mich von allen Lasterbeulen völlig zu heilen, lässt er sich verwunden.	*From the ropes of my sins* *me to set free,* *is my Savior bound.* *Me from all sin's bruises* *fully to heal,* *he allows himself to be wounded.*

Est ist vollbracht *[It is the end]*

From Part II (no. 58), the aria is scored for viola da gamba, strings, bassoon, and continuo. This is a free text, drawn from the Postel libretto cited above. The aria's subject is the last moments of Jesus' mortal life.

Est ist vollbracht, O Trost vor die gekränkten Seelen, die Trauer nacht, lässt mich die letze Stunde zählen. Der Held aus Juda siegt mit Macht, und schliesst den Kampf.	*It is finished,* *O comfort for the ailing souls,* *the night of sorrow,* *allows me the final hour to count.* *The hero of Judah triumphs with might,* *and concludes the battle.*

PASSIO SECUNDUM MATTHÆUM

(Matthäus-Passion/St. Matthew Passion)
BWV 244
1727 or 1729
libretto by Picander, a pseudonym for Christian Friedrich Henrici (1700-1764); it is probable that the free text poems only were by Henrici (free text refers to poetry that is not a paraphrase or adaptation directly from Scripture), with biblical narrative from the Gospel of Matthew and some chorale texts by the composer

The date of first performance of the Passion is in dispute, occuring at Thomaskirche, Leipzig, on either April 11, 1727 or April 15, 1729. A revised version was performed March 30, 1736. A Passion is a musical setting of Jesus' sufferings and death as related by one of the four Gospel writers.

Buss und Reu *[Grief and pain]*

From Part I (nos. 9-10), scored for flutes and continuo; the aria is a free text.

Du lieber Heiland du, wenn deine Jünger töricht streiten, dass dieses fromme Weib mit Salben deinen Leib zum Grabe will bereiten; so lasse mir inzwischen zu, von meiner Augen Tränenflüssen ein Wasser auf dein Haupt zu giessen.	*You, beloved Savior,* *when your disciples foolishly quarrel,* *because this devout woman* *with ointment your body* *for the grave will prepare;* *so allow in the meantime,* *from my eyes* *a flood of tears* *on your head to shower.*
Buss und Reu knirscht das Sündenherz entzwei, dass die Tropfen meiner Zähren angenehme Spezerei, treuer Jesu, dir gebähren.	*Repentance and regret* *grind the sinful heart asunder,* *as the drops* *of my tears a pleasant spice,* *faithful Jesus, you bring forth.*

Erbarme dich, mein Gott *[Have mercy, Lord]*

From Part II (no. 47), scored for solo vioin, strings, and continuo; a free text that comes after Peter's third denial in the structure of the Passion.

Erbarme dich, mein Gott,	*Have mercy on me, my God,*
um meiner Zähren willen;	*for the sake of my tears;*
schaue hier,	*look here,*
Herz und Auge weinte vor dir bitterlich.	*heart and eyes weep for you bitterly.*

Können Tränen meiner Wangen *[If my tears be unavailing]*

From Part II (nos. 60-61), scored for strings and continuo; a free text, commenting on the scourging of Jesus.

Erbarm es Gott!	*Have mercy God!*
Hier steht der Heiland angebunden.	*Here stands the Savior bound.*
O Geisselung,	*Oh scourges,*
o Schläg',	*oh beatings,*
o Wunden!	*o wounds!*
Ihr Henker, haltet ein!	*Exceutioner, stop!*
Erweichet euch der Seelen Schmerz,	*Do you not soften at the soul's pain,*
der Anblick solches Jammers nicht?	*at the sight of such misery?*
Ach ja, ihr habt ein Herz,	*O yes, you have a heart,*
das muss der Martersäule gleich	*that must like the torture support [cross]*
und noch viel härter sein.	*and still much harder be.*
Erbarmt euch,	*Have pity,*
haltet ein!	*Stop!*
Können Tränen meiner Wangen	*Can tears of my cheeks*
nichts erlangen,	*not reach you,*
o, so nehmt mein Herz hinein!	*o, so take my heart away!*
Aber lasst es bei den Fluten,	*But leave it near the floods,*
wenn die Wunden milde bluten,	*when the tender wounds gently bleed,*
auch die Opferschale sein.	*also a chalice for the victim's blood to be.*

WEIHNACHTS-ORATORIUM

(Christmas Oratorio)
BWV 248
1734-1735
text attributed to Picander, a pseudonym for Christian Friedrich Henrici (1700-1764); based on Luke 2:1, 3-12, and Matthew 1:1-12 (the Luther German Bible)

The Weihnachts-Oratorium is actually a collection of six individual church cantatas, designed to be performed at each of the six church events between Christmas and Epiphany. The piece contains newly composed music, and adaptations from three secular cantatas (BWV 213-215). The first cantata was first performed on Christmas Day, 1734 at Thomaskirche, Leipzig. The remaining cantatas followed in order on the second and third days following Christmas, on New Year's Day (Feast of the Circumcision), on the Sunday after New Year, and on the Feast of the Epiphany. Performances took place at both Thomaskirche and Nikolaikirche, Leipzig.

Bereite dich, Zion *[Prepare thyself, Zion]*

From Part I (the first cantata), Christmas Day.

Nun wird mein liebster Bräutigam,	*Now will my dearest bridegroom,*
nun wird der Held	*now will the hero*
aus Davids Stamm zum Trost,	*of David's stem for the comfort,*
zum Heil der Erden	*and salvation of the world*
einmal geboren werden.	*finally be born.*
Nun wird der Stern	*Now will the star*
aus Jakob scheinen,	*of Jacob shine,*
sein Strahl bricht schon hervor;	*his radiance breaks forth already;*
auf, Zion!	*up, Zion!*

und verlasse nun das Weinen, dein Wohl steigt hoch empor.	*and leave nosw the weeping, your well-being ascends aloft.*
Bereite dich, Zion, mit zärtlichen Trieben den Schönsten, den Liebsten bald bei dir zu sehn. Deine Wangen müssen heut viel schöner prangen, eile, den Bräutigam sehnlichst zu lieben.	*Prepare yourself, Zion, with tender emotion the fairest, the dearest soon with you to see. Your cheeks must today with much beauty be resplendant, hurry, the Bridegroom longing to love.*

Schlafe, mein Liebster — ***[Slumber, beloved]***

From Part II (the second cantata), Second Christmas Day. The music for this aria was taken from Cantata No. 213, *Hercules auf dem Scheidewege* (1733).

Schlafe, mein Liebster, geniesse der Ruh, wache nach diesem vor aller Gedeihen! Labe die Brust, empfinde die Lust, wo wir unser Herz erfreuen!	*Sleep, my dearest, enjoy the peace, watch after this over the well-being of all! Refresh the breast, feel the joy, where we our hearts gladden!*

Schliesse, mein Herze — ***[Keep, O my spirit]***

From Part III (the third cantata), Third Christmas Day.

Schliesse, mein Herze, dies selige Wunder fest in deinem Glauben ein! Lasse dies Wunder die göttlichen Werke immer zur Stärke deines schwachen Glaubens sein!	*Lock, my heart, this blessed wonder firm in your belief! Let the wonder of the Godly works always the strength of your weak faith be!*

Antonín Dvořák
1841-1904

STABAT MATER
Opus 58
1880
text is traditional Latin from the Roman Catholic liturgy, a 13th century sequence attributed to the Franciscan Jacopone da Todi

Composed 1875-1878. First performed in Prague, March 16, 1880. Stabat Mater (literally translated as "mother standing") refers to Mary standing at the base of the cross. The text of the Stabat Mater is still used in the Roman Catholic Church for the Feast of the Seven Sorrows (September 15).

Inflammatus et accensus

Inflammatus et accensus Per te, Virgo, sim defensus In die judicii. Fac me cruce custodiri, Morte Christi præmuniri, Confoveri gratia.	*Inflamed and in flames Through the Virgin I am defended in the day of judgement. May I by the cross be guarded, by the death of Christ made safe, by Thy eternal grace.*

George Frideric Handel
1685-1759

DIXIT DOMINUS
1707
text is Psalm 109 from the Vulgate (the 4th century, Roman Catholic authorized Roman Catholic Latin translation of the Bible), which is Psalm 110 in the Protestant Bible; added to the Psalm text is the Lesser Doxology "Gloria patri et Filio"

Composed in April of 1707 in Rome, and though no record exists, believed to have been first performed there around that time. "Virgam virtutis tuae" is the second of eight movements.

Virgam virtutis tuae

Virgam virtutis tuae	*Virtuous Virgin, you*
emitet Dominus ex Sion:	*sent forth the God of Zion:*
dominare in medio	*to rule in our midst*
inimicorum tuorum.	*among his enemies.*

JUDAS MACCABÆUS
1747
libretto by Thomas Morell (1703-1784), based on the book of the Maccabees and the 12th book of Josephus' *Antiquities of the Jews*

Commissioned by Frederic, Prince of Wales. Composed July 8 or 9 through August 11, 1746. First performed at the Theatre Royal at Covent Garden, London, April 1, 1747. Revisions and additions were made for frequent new productions, in 1748, then annually from 1750 through 1759. The oratorio relates the restoration of liberty to the Jews under leader Judas Maccabæus.

Father of Heav'n!

The aria opens Act III, and is a prayer of blessing sung by the character of the Priest.

MESSIAH
1742
text by Charles Jennens (1700-1773), drawn from various biblical sources and the Prayer Book Psalter

Composed between August 22 and September 12, 1741. First performed April 13, 1742 at the Music Hall on Fishamble Street, Dublin. The performance was a benefit for several of the city's charities. The libretto is drawn from the Prophets, the Gospels, the Pauline Epistles, and Revelation, detailing the prophecy of Christ's coming, his life, death, resurrection, promise of second coming, and the response of believers. *Messiah* is theological in nature, not the more common dramatic Handelian oratorio. The soloists are impersonal, and the chorus assumes an expanded role as commentators. Many changes and additions were made in the oratorio, with 13 revisions of the score in the years 1743-1759. Many of the solo movements were sometimes sung by different voice types in different versions and keys, a practice the composer directed. Contralto Susanna Maria Cibber, sister to Thomas Arne, was the performer of the alto arias at the premiere of *Messiah* in Dublin.

But who may abide

From Part I. The text is from Malachi 3:2. The version presented here, the aria in its most familiar form, came from a 1750 revision for the castrato alto Gaetano Guadagni. The aria was originally for bass, and without the *prestissimo* section.

O thou that tellest good tidings to Zion

From Part I. The text for the recitative is drawn from Isaiah 7:14 and Matthew 1:23. The aria's text comes from Isaiah 40:9 and Isaiah 60:1. The chorus continues the number at the conclusion of the solo. This movement was not rewritten in new versions subsequent to the original.

He was despised

From Part II. The text is from Isaiah 53:1, 3, 6. Handel never rewrote this movement, and except for some discrepancies in text underlay, it remains largely as it was at the first performance in 1742 (although at times it was transposed for other voices).

Thou art gone up on high

From Part II. The text is from Psalm 68:18. This is a revised version of the aria for alto, originally for bass. The second version (1750) was for the castrato alto Gaetano Guadagni. There was yet another version of the aria composed, this time for soprano. The Guadagni version became the standard one used. This aria is often cut in performances of *Messiah.*

Franz Joseph Haydn

1832-1809

STABAT MATER

1767
text is traditional Latin from the Roman Catholic liturgy, a 13th century sequence attributed to the Franciscan Jacopone da Todi

Composed 1767, Eszterháza. No record of a performance exists from around that time, but the work was performed in the 1770s at Piaristenkirche in Vienna, conducted by the composer. Stabat Mater (literally translated as "mother standing") refers to Mary standing at the base of the cross. The text of the Stabat Mater is still used in the Roman Catholic Church for the Feast of the Seven Sorrows (September 15).

Fac me vere tecum flere

Fac me vere tecum flere	*Let me truly with you weep*
crucifixo condolere,	*and torment suffer severely,*
donec ego vixero.	*as long as I live.*
Juxta crucem tecum stare,	*By the cross with you stay*
et me tibi sociare	*I with you united*
in planctu desidero.	*in lamaentation grieve for you.*

Felix Mendelssohn

1809-1847

ELIJAH

(Elias)
Opus 70
1846
libretto by Julius Schubring, after I Kings 17-19, II Kings 2, and other biblical passages; English libretto by William Bartholomew

Composed summer of 1846. First performed August 26, 1846, at the Birmingham Festival, England. William Bartholomew was given the *Elijah* libretto in the middle of May, 1846, and was engaged to translate it into English for the August premiere, receiving sections as they were completed. Mendelssohn and Schubring had used Luther's translation of the Bible, interpolating and paraphrasing liberally. Bartholomew's task was not only to translate, but also to make the text agree with the King James Bible. He added the following disclaimer to the libretto of *Elijah:* "The author of this English version has endeavored to render it as nearly in accordance with the Scriptural Texts as the Music to which it is adapted will admit: the references are therefore to be considered rather as authorities than quotations." The arias are presented in both English, the language of the premiere, and German, the working language of Mendelssohn's composition. It may be assumed that the composer intended for English speaking audiences to hear the piece in the vernacular.

Woe unto them who forsake Him *[Weh ihnen, dass sie von mir weichen]*

From Part I, following Elijah's fiery sermon-aria "Is not his word like a fire?"

O rest in the Lord *[Sei stille dem Herrn]*

From Part II. The angel appears, encouraging the downcast Elijah to persevere.

Wolfgang Amadeus Mozart

1756-1791

MASS IN C MINOR

K. 427 (417a)
1783
text is the traditional Latin Mass from the Roman Catholic liturgy

The "Grand" (or "Great") Mass in C minor was first performed October 26, 1783 at St. Peter's Abbey, Salzburg. Left incomplete at the time of the premiere, Mozart perhaps filled in the missing sections with parts of earlier mass settings, or perhaps they were sung as chant in the performance. The composer never completed the work. There is no Agnus Dei. Only the "Et incarnatus est" exists of the Credo section. The Sanctus section is fragmentary.

Laudamus te

The edition that appears in this volume may not be familiar to some. The Breitkopf & Härtel edition that was published in 1901, edited by Alois Schmitt, often reprinted (it is the G. Schirmer edition in use in the U.S.), contains an abridged version of the movement. The Schmitt edition was the only edition available for several decades. The edition in this anthology is based on the autograph full score.

The role is for a second soprano, but may be sung by a mezzo-soprano. The range of the "Laudamus te" is significantly higher than most of the other selections in the alto collection, and in the opinion of the editor, is a welcome addition to the alto volume. (This movement has also been included in the soprano volume of this anthology.)

Laudamus te,	*We praise Thee,*
benediciums te,	*we bless thee,*
adoramus te,	*we adore Thee,*
glorificamus te.	*we glorify Thee.*

Giovanni Battista Pergolesi

1710-1736

STABAT MATER

1736
text is traditional Latin from the Roman Catholic liturgy, a 13th century sequence attributed to the Franciscan Jacopone da Todi

First performed March 17, 1736, Naples. Traditionally believed to have been commissioned by the Confraternity of San Luigi di Palazzo, Naples, although there is evidence that shows Duke Marzio Domenico IV Carafa Maddaloni as the patron. Stabat Mater (literally translated as "mother standing") refers to Mary standing at the base of the cross. The text of the Stabat Mater is still used in the Roman Catholic Church for the Feast of the Seven Sorrows (September 15).

Quæ mœrebat et dolebat

Quæ mœrebatet dolebat,	*Who mourns and suffers pain,*
et tremebat dum videbat	*and trembles at the sight*
nati pœnas inclyti.	*of her child bent in punishment.*

Eija, mater, fons amoris

Eija, mater, fons amoris,	*Oh, mother, fountain of love,*
me sentire vim doloris;	*I experience anguish;*
fac, ut tecum lugeam.	*allow me to mourn with you.*

Fac ut portem

Fac ut portem Christi mortem, passionis fac consortem, et plagas recolere. Fac me plagis vulnerari, cruce hac inebriari, ob amorem filii.	*Allow me, as bearer of Christ's death, allow me his suffering to share, and wounds recall. Let me with his wounds be stricken, with his torment be saturated, because of love for the Son.*

Henry Purcell
1659-1695

TE DEUM LAUDAMUS
1694
text is a traditional hymn of praise, originally in Latin, formerly attributed to St. Ambrose, but possibly written by the 6th century bishop Nicetus, with some lines taken from De mortalitate (A.D. 272) of St. Cyprian

This, along with the companion Jubilate Deo, was written for St. Cecilia's Day, November 22, 1694. St. Cecilia is celebrated as the patron saint of music. The Te Deum is used in Latin in the Roman Catholic liturgy, often replacing the last responsory of Matins on feast days and Sundays, and in English in the Anglican church as one of the canticles of Morning Prayer. It is also sung as a hymn on various occasions, particularly as a thanksgiving.

Vouchsafe, O Lord

Gioachino Rossini
1792-1868

MESSE SOLENNELLE
1864
text is the traditional Latin Mass from the Roman Catholic liturgy

Composed in 1863, first performed in Paris, March 14, 1864, for the dedication of the private chapel of Countess Louise Pillet-Will. This original version was for 4 soloists, a chorus of 8 voices, 2 pianos and harmonium. The piece is often called "Petite Messe Solennelle," referring to the chamber music scale of the design, not because of brevity or liturgical reasons. Revised in 1867 for full orchestra. This second version was performed in Paris at the Théâtre-Italien, February 24, 1869.

Agnus Dei

Agnus Dei qui tollis peccata mundi, miserere nobis.	*Lamb of God who takes away the sins of the world, have mercy upon us.*
Agnus Dei qui tollis peccata mundi dona nobis pacem.	*Lamb of God who takes away the sins of the world give us peace.*

STABAT MATER

1832; 1842

text is traditional Latin from the Roman Catholic liturgy, a 13th century sequence attributed to the Franciscan Jacopone da Todi

First performed on Good Friday, 1833 at Cappella di San Filippo El Real, Madrid. Due to illness, Rossini requested that Giovanni Tadolini compose six of the twelve sections in order to complete the work for the premiere. In 1841 Rossini replaced the six Tadolini movements with new composition. The revised Stabat Mater was first performed January 7, 1842 at the Théâtre Italien, Paris. Stabat Mater (literally translated as "mother standing") refers to Mary standing at the base of the cross. The text of the Stabat Mater is still used in the Roman Catholic Church for the Feast of the Seven Sorrows (September 15).

Fac ut portem

Fac ut portem Christi mortem,
passionis ejus sortem
et plagas recolere.
Fac me plagis vulnerari,
cruce hac inebriari,
ob amorem filii.

Allow me as bearer of Christ's death,
his suffering to share
and wounds recall.
Let me with his wounds be stricken,
with his torment be saturated,
because of love for the Son.

Giuseppe Verdi

1813-1901

MESSA DI REQUIEM

1874

text is the traditional Latin Requiem Mass from the Roman Catholic liturgy; Requiem ("rest") is a Mass for the dead

The piece has a long history of development. In November, 1868, Verdi sent his publisher, Ricordi, a letter proposing a Requiem Mass, written by Italian composers, to honor Rossini, who had died early in the month. There was to be one performance only, on the first anniversary of Rossini's death, and no one was to profit from the work. Verdi was assigned the "Libera me" section of the mass, and completed composition in August. Severe conflicts and controversies prevented the "Rossini Requiem" from being presented. (It wasn't heard until 1988 at the Parma Cathedral.) In 1873 the Italian novelist Alessandro Manzoni died. Verdi proposed to Ricordi that he would write a Requiem in honor of Manzoni, and like the "Rossini Requiem," wanted to have the first performance on the first anniversary of Manzoni's death. Verdi incorporated the "Libera me" section that he had composed five years earlier. The Messa di Requiem was first performed May 22, 1874 at the Church of San Marco, Milan. The "Liber scriptus" was revised, and first performed in May of 1875 in the new version (presented in the anthology). This is the only movement to have any significant revision subsequent to the 1874 premiere.

Liber scriptus

Liber scriptus proferetur,
In quo totum continetur,
Unde mundus, judicetur.
Judex ergo cum sedebit,
Quid quid latet apparebit,
Nil inultum remanebit.

The book of scriptures revealed,
wherein everything is contained,
from whence comes the world's judgement.
The judge therefore is seated,
indeed, at last things hidden are made known,
nothing unavenged remains.

Antonio Vivaldi

1669-1741

MAGNIFICAT

RV 610a-611

text taken from Luke 1:46-55, from the Vulgate (the 4th century, authorized Roman Catholic Latin translation of the Bible); besides these verses a Magnificat (the canticle of the Virgin) traditionally includes two additional verses of the Lesser Doxology "Gloria Patri et Filio"

There is no clear chronology known for Vivaldi's sacred works, and no date has been theorized for the Magnificat.

Esurientes implevit

This aria is one of five found in Vivaldi's manuscript, apparently written specifically for particular singers, replacing the original movements in the Magnificat. This "Esurientes implevit" was composed for a contralto by the name of Ambrosina. In the first version, this movement is a duet for 2 sopranos.

Esurientes implevit bonis et divites dimisit inanes.	*He has filled the hungry with good things* *and the rich sent away empty.*

GLORIA

RV 589

text is the traditional Gloria section from the Latin Mass of the Roman Catholic liturgy

This is the second of two D major Glorias composed by Vivaldi. No exact chronology of Vivaldi's sacred works exists, but both Glorias are believed to have been written after 1708. The first modern performance of this Gloria took place in Siena, Italy, in 1939.

Qui sedes ad dexteram Patris

Qui sedes ad dexteram Patris, miserere nobis.	*Who sits on the right hand of the Father,* *have mercy upon us.*

The Arias

Agnus Dei

from

MASS IN B MINOR

Johann Sebastian Bach

[f]
tr
4
7
p
A - gnus _ De -
10
- i qui tol - lis pec - ca - ta mun -

13
di, qui tol - lis pec - ca - ta, pec - ca - ta mun - di, mi - se - re -
16
- re no - bis, mi - se - re - re no - bis,
f
19
mi - se - re - re no - bis, qui tol - lis pec -
21
ca - ta, pec - ca - ta mun - di, mi - se - re - re no - bis.

24
27
A - gnus _ De - i qui tol - lis pec-ca - ta _ mun - di,
p
31
a - gnus _ De - i qui tol - lis pec - ca -
34
- ta, qui tol - lis pec - ca - ta. Pec-ca - ta mun - di, qui tol - lis pec -

37
ca - ta,
mi - se - re - re, qui tol - lis pec - ca - ta, mi - se - re - re
40
no - bis, mi - se - re - re no - bis, mi - se - re - re no -
43
bis, mi - se - re - re no - bis, mi-se - re - re no - bis.
46

Qui sedes ad dextram Patris

from

MASS IN B MINOR

Johann Sebastian Bach

[Andante]
*
[f]

4
tr
p
f

8

11

*Play small size notes in the absence of an oboe.

14
17
Qui se - -
21
- des ad dex-tram Pa-tris, qui se - - -
25
- des ad dex - tram Pa-tris, ad dex - tram Pa - tris,

29
mi - se-re - re no - bis!
f
33
p f
37
41
Qui se -
p

45
- - des ad dex - tram Pa - tris, mi -
tr
48
- se - re - re no-bis, qui se -
52
- des - ad dex - tram Pa - tris, mi - se - re - re
56
no - bis,
f

60
p f
64
mi - se - re - re no - bis, mi - se - re - re
tr
p
68
no - bis, qui se - - - -
71
Adagio
- des ad dex - tram Pa - tris, mi - se - re - re

74
[a tempo]
tr
no - bis, qui se - - - -
tr
p
77
- - - - - des_ ad dex - tram
80
Pa - tris, mi - se - re - re_____ no - bis!
f
83

Qui sedes ad dextram Patris
from
MASS IN B MINOR

Johann Sebastian Bach

Oboe d'amore

[*f*]

tr

5

9

12

15

18

p

23

27

f

31

35

39

The part may be carefully cut from the book.

42
p
46
50
54
f
58
62
p
66
tr
69
73
Adagio
tr
[a tempo]
77
80
f
83

Von den Stricken meiner Sünden

(From the shackles of my transgressions)

from

PASSIO SECUNDUM JOANNEM

(St. John Passion)

Johann Sebastian Bach

[Andante]
[f]

6
Von den ___ Stric -
From the ___ shack - les ___
tr
p

11
- ken _ mei - ner _ Sün - den ___ mich zu ent - bin - den, mich zu ent - bin -
_ of _ my _ trans - gres - sions, ___ to grant me free - dom, to grant me free -

15
tr
- den, wird mein Heil _ ge - bun - den;
- dom, is the high _ Sa - vior bound.
f
19
tr
Von den Stric - ken
From the shack - les
p
tr
23
mei - ner Sün - den mich zu ent - bin - den, mich zu ent - bin -
of my trans - gres - sions, to grant me free - dom, to grant me free -
tr

27
- den, wird mein Heil ge - bun - den, von den Stric - ken
- dom, is the high Sa - vior bound. From the shack - les
31
mei - ner Sün - den mich zu ent - bin - den,
of my trans - gres - sions to grant me free - dom,
35
mich zu ent - bin - den, mich zu ent - bin - den, wird mein Heil ge - bun -
to grant me free - dom, to grant me free - dom, is the high Sa - vior

39
den.
bound.
f
44
Mich von al - len
From my ach - ing
tr
p
49
La - ster - beu - len völ - lig zu hei - len,
wounds and bruis - es, ful - ly to heal me,

53
völ-lig zu hei - len,
ful - ly to heal me,
mich von al - len
from my ach - ing
57
La - ster - beu - len
wounds and bruis - es,
völ - lig,
ful - ly,
völ - lig,
ful - ly,
61
völ - lig zu hei - len, völ - lig zu hei - len, völ-lig zu hei - len, lässt er sich
ful - ly to heal me, ful - ly to heal me, ful - ly to heal me, was He bruised

65
ver - wun - den.
and wound - ed.
f
70
Von den Stric - ken,
From the shack - les,
von den
from the
p
74
Stric - ken mei - ner Sün - den mich zu ent - bin -
shack - les of my trans - gres - sions, to grant me free -

78
den, mich zu ent - bin - den, wird mein Heil _ ge - bun - den;
dom, to grant me free - dom is the high _ Sa - vior bound.
tr
f
82
von den
From the
tr
p
86
Stric - ken, von den Stric - ken
shack - les, from the shack - les
tr
tr

90
mei - ner Sün - den mich zu ent - bin - den, mich zu ent - bin -
of my trans - gres - sions, to grant me free - dom, to grant me free -
tr
94
- den, wird mein Heil ge - bun - den, von den Stric - ken
- dom, is the high Sa - vior bound, from the shack - les,
98
mei - ner Sün - den mich zu ent - bin - den,
of my trans - gres - sions, to grant me free - dom,

102
mich zu ent - bin - den, mich zu ent - bin - den, wird mein Heil ge - bun -
to grant me free - dom, to grant me free - dom, is the high Sa - vior
106
den.
bound.
f
110
tr

Es ist vollbracht

(It is the end)
from
PASSIO SECUNDUM JOANNEM
(St. John Passion)

Johann Sebastian Bach

Molto Adagio

3
tr

5
Es ist voll - bracht, es ist voll - bracht, o Trost für
It is the ___ end, it is the ___ end, oh com - fort
p

7
die ge - kränk - ten See - len, o Trost, o Trost! es is voll -
for all wear - y spir - its, oh rest oh rest! It is the
9
tr
bracht, o Trost für die ge-kränk-ten See - len,
end, oh rest for all the wear - y spir - its,
tr
11
die Trau - er - nacht,
this grief - filled night,

13
die Trau - er - nacht
this grief - filled night,
läßt mich die letz - te
un - veils the fi - nal
15
tr
Stun - de, die letz - te Stun - de zäh - len,
hour, the fi - nal hour draw - ing;
16
tr
die Trau - er - nacht läßt mich die letz-te Stun - de zäh - len.
this grief - filled night un-veils the fi-nal hour draw - ing.

18
Der
Now
20
Alla breve
Held aus Ju - da siegt mit Macht,
Ju - dah's he - ro fights the fight,
der Held aus Ju - da
now Ju - dah's he - ro
tr
f
p
23
siegt mit Macht,
fights the fight,
der Held aus Ju - da siegt mit Macht,
now Ju - dah's he - ro fights the fight,
tr
f
p
f

26
und schliesst den Kampf,
and ends with might,
und schliesst den Kampf,
and ends with might,
p
29
und schliesst den Kampf,
and ends with might.
32
der Held aus Ju - da siegt mit Macht,
Now Ju - dah's he - ro fights the fight,
der
now
tr
f
p

35
Held aus Ju - da siegt mit Macht,
Ju - dah's he - ro fights the fight,
tr
tr
38
Adagio
und schliesst den Kampf, und schliesst den Kampf. Es ist voll - bracht!
and ends with might, and ends with might. It is the end.
f
41
43
Es ist voll - bracht!
It is the end.
tr

Buss und Reu

(Grief and pain)

from

PASSIO SECUNDUM MATTHÆUM

(St. Matthew Passion)

Recit.

Johann Sebastian Bach

[Adagio]
Du lie - ber Hei - land du, wenn dei - ne
O bless - ed Sav - iour, grant, though these may
[p]
(Bass pizz.)
3
Jün - ger tör - icht strei - ten, dass die - ses from - me Weib mit
in - dig - na - tion have, be - cause this wo - man's care with
5
Sal - ben dei - nen Leib zum Gra - be will be - rei - ten; so
oint - ment would pre - pare Thy Bod - y for the grave; Yea,

7
las - se mir in - zwi - schen zu, von mei - ner Au - gen Trä - nen - flüs - sen ein Was - ser
this we ask for, this we want, that we, our eyes with tears o'er - flow - ing, may pen - i -
9
auf dein Haupt zu gies - sen.
tence un - feigned be show - ing.
Aria
[Andante]
[mf]
6

13
Buss _ und Reu, Buss ___ und Reu knirscht das __ Sün - den -
Grief _ and pain, grief ___ and pain rend re - pent - ing ___
[p]
19
herz ent - zwei,
hearts in twain,
f
24
Buss _ und
grief _ and
p
30
Reu, _ Buss _ und Reu _ knirscht ___ das Sün - den - herz ent -
pain, _ grief _ and pain _ rend ______ re - pent - ing hearts in

36
zwei, knirscht das Sün - den - herz ent - zwei, Buss und
twain, rend re - pent - ing hearts in twain, grief and
42
Reu, Buss und Reu knirscht das Sün - den - herz ent -
pain, grief and pain rend re - pent - ing hearts in
48
zwei, Buss und Reu knirscht
twain, grief and pain rend
54
das Sün - den - herz ent - zwei,
re - pent - ing hearts in twain.
f

60
66
[𝄐]
dass die Trop - fen mei - ner
May the an - guish of my
*
[𝄐]
Fine
[𝄐]
p
72
Zäh - ren an - ge - neh - me Spe - ze - rei,
spir - it in Thy sight ac - cept - ance gain,
78
treu - er Je - su, dir ge - bäh - ren,
Lord, Thy fa - vor I would mer - it.
f

*fermatas at Fine

84
dass die Trop - fen mei - ner
May the an - guish of my
p
89
Zäh - ren an - ge - neh - me Spe - ze - rei, treu - er
spir - it in Thy sight ac - cept - ance gain, Lord, Thy
94
Je - - - su, dir ge - bäh - ren,
fa - - - vor I would mer - it,
100
tr
D.C. al Fine
treu - er Je - su, treu - er Je - su, dir ge - bäh - ren.
Lord, Thy fa - vor, Lord, Thy fa - vor I would mer - it.

Können Tränen meiner Wangen

(If my tears be unavailing)

from

PASSIO SECUNDUM MATTHÆUM

(St. Matthew Passion)

Recit.

Johann Sebastian Bach

[Larghetto]
p
Er - barm - es Gott! Hier steht der Heil-and an - ge - bun - den. O
O gra - cious God, be - hold, and see the Sav-ior bound: Now
[p]
[sim.]

3
Geis - se - lung, o Schläg', o Wun - den! Ihr Hen - ker, hal - tet
scourge they Him, and smite, and wound. Tor - ment - ors, stay your

5
ein! Er - wei - chet euch der See - len Schmerz, der An - blick
hands! It should more gen - tle thoughts im - part, to see such

Copyright © 1994 by HAL LEONARD CORPORATION
International Copyright Secured All Rights Reserved

7
sol - ches Jam - mers nicht? Ach ja, ihr habt ein Herz, das muss der
an - guish meek - ly borne. But no, with you the heart from sweet com -
9
Mar - ter - säu - le gleich und noch viel här - ter sein. Er -
pas - sion turns with scorn, and all un - yield - ing stands. Have
11
barmt euch, hal - tet ein!
pit - y, stay your hands!
Aria
[Andante]
[mf]
[sim.]

Kön-nen Trä - nen mei-ner Wan - gen nichts er-lang - en,
If my tears be un-a - vail - ing, vain my wail - ing,
nichts er - lang - en, o, so nehmt mein Herz hin - ein,
vain my wail - ing, take the ver - y heart of me,

21
_ so _ nehmt mein Herz _ hin - ein, __ o, __ so __ nehmt mein Herz hin - ein!
_ the _ ver - y heart _ of me, __ take _ the __ ver - y heart of me.
25
29
33
Kön - nen _ Trä - nen mei - ner _ Wan - gen nichts er - lang -
If my _ tears ____ be un - a - vail - ing, vain my _ wail -
p

36
- en, kön - nen Trä - nen mei - ner Wan - gen
- ing, if my tears be un - a - vail - ing,
39
nichts er - lang - en, kön - nen Trä - nen mei - ner Wan-gen
vain my wail - ing, if my tears be un - a - vail - ing,
43
nichts er - lang - en, o, so nehmt mein Herz hin -
vain my wail - ing, take the ver - y heart of
46
ein, so nehmt mein Herz, mein Herz hin - ein, o, so nehmt mein Herz, o,
me, the ver - y heart, the heart of me, take the ver - y heart, take

50
_ so _ nehmt mein Herz hin - ein!
_ the _ ver - y heart of me.
f
54
58
62
A - ber _ lasst _ es bei den _ Flu - ten,
That my _ heart, _ tho' fails my _ plead - ing,
Fine
p
*

*fermatas for Fine

wenn die _ Wun - den mil - de _ blu - ten, auch die _ Op-fer - scha - le sein.
when the _ sa - cred wounds are _ bleed - ing, may a __ ver - y chal - ice be.

A - ber _ lasst ________ es bei ___ den _ Flu - ten, _ wenn __ die __ Wun - den _
That my _ heart, ________ tho' fails ___ my _ plead - ing, _ when __ the __ sa - cred _

81
mil - de _ blu - ten, _ auch die _ Op-fer - scha-le sein, die Op - fer - scha - le, die Op-fer -
wounds _ are _ bleed-ing, _ may a ___ ver - y chal-ice be, a ver - y chal - ice, a ver - y
85
scha - le sein. ___ A - ber _ lasst ___ es bei den _ Flu - ten,
chal - ice be. ___ That my _ heart, ___ tho' fails my _ plead - ing,
88
D.C. al Fine
wenn die _ Wun - den mil - de blu - ten, auch die _ Op - fer - scha - le sein.
when the _ sa - cred wounds are bleed - ing, May a ___ ver - y chal - ice be.

Erbarme dich, mein Gott
(Have mercy, Lord)
from
PASSIO SECUNDUM MATTHÆUM
(St. Matthew Passion)

Johann Sebastian Bach

[Largo]
*
p
(pizz.)
3
tr
5
7
Er -
Have
tr

*Play small size notes in the absence of a violin. The bass line may also be played by a solo cello.

9
bar - me dich, er - bar - me dich, mein Gott, um
mer - cy, Lord, have mer - cy, Lord, on me, re -
11
mei - ner Zäh - - ren wil - len, er -
gard my bit - - ter weep - ing, have
13
bar - me dich, er - bar - me dich, mein Gott, er -
mer - cy Lord, have mer - cy, Lord, on me, have

15
bar - - me, er - bar - me dich um
mer - - cy, have mer - cy, Lord, re -
17
mei - ner Zäh - ren, um mei - ner Zäh - ren wil - len,
gard my weep - ing, re - gard my bit - ter weep - ing,
19
er - bar - me dich, mein Gott, um mei - ner
have mer - cy, Lord, on me, re - gard my

21
Zäh - - - ren, um mei - ner Zäh - ren wil - len;
weep - - - ing, re - gard my bit - ter weep - ing.
23
25
schau - e
Look on
27
hier, schau - e hier, Herz und
me, look on me, heart and

29
Au - ge weint vor dir, weint vor dir bit - ter -
eyes both weep to Thee, weep to Thee bit - ter -
31
lich. Er - bar - me dich, er - bar - me dich,
ly. Have mer - cy, Lord, have mer - cy, Lord,
33
er - bar - me dich, mein Gott, um
have mer - cy, Lord, on me, re -

35
mei - ner Zäh - - ren wil - len, er -
gard my bit - - ter weep - ing, have
37
bar - me dich, er - bar - me dich, mein Gott, er -
mer - cy, Lord, have mer - cy, Lord, on me, have
39
bar - - me, er - bar - me dich, um
mer - - cy, have mer - cy, Lord, re -

41
mei - ner Zäh - ren, um mei - ner Zäh - ren wil - len,
gard my weep - ing, re - gard my bit - ter weep - ing,
43
er - bar - me dich, mein Gott, um mei - ner
have mer - cy, Lord, on me, re - gard my
45
Zäh - - - ren, um mei - ner Zäh-ren wil - len.
weep - - ing, re - gard my bit - ter weep - ing.
f
[colla voce]

47
f

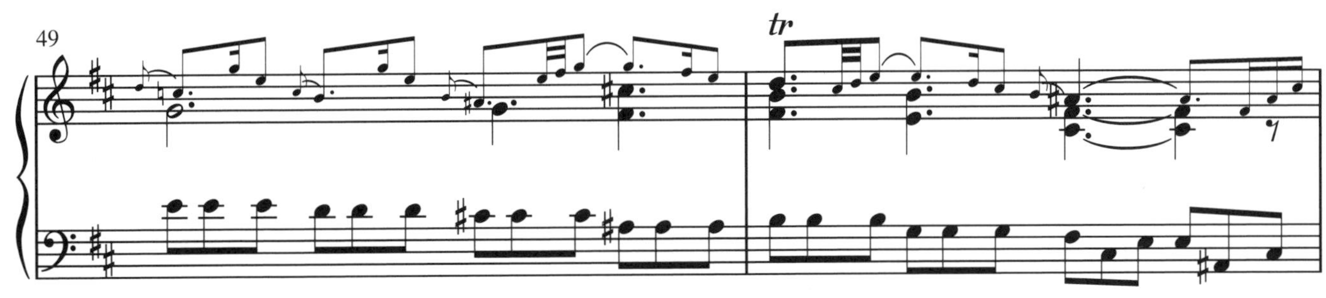
49
tr

51

53
tr

Erbarme dich, mein Gott

(Have mercy, Lord)

from

PASSIO SECUNDUM MATTHÆUM

(St. Matthew Passion)

Johann Sebastian Bach

[Largo]
Violin
tr
tr

The part may be carefully cut from the book.

18
20
21
22
f
25
tr
27
30
32
35
37

40
42
44
45
46
49
51
52
53
54
tr
tr

Bereite dich, Zion

(Prepare thyself, Zion)
from
WEIHNACHTS-ORATORIUM
(Christmas Oratorio)

Johann Sebastian Bach

Recit.
Nun wird mein lieb - ster Bräu - ti-gam, nun wird der
Be - hold the Bride-groom, full of grace, be - hold the
3
Held aus Da - vids Stamm zum Trost, zum Heil der Er - den ein - mal ge - bo - ren
Hope of Da - vid's race, to save and heal the earth doth stoop to mor - tal
6
wer-den. Nun wird der Stern aus Ja - kob schei-nen, sein Strahl bricht schon her - vor; auf,
birth. Be - hold the Star of Ja - cob shin - ing, its bright-ness fills the sky. Wake

9
Zi - on! und ver-las - se nun das Wei-nen, dein Wohl steigt hoch em - por.
Zi - on! and for-get thy sad re - pin - ing, thy Hope comes from on high.
Aria
[Allegretto]
tr
[f]
7
13
Be - rei - te dich, Zi - on, mit
Pre - pare thy - self, Zi - on, with
p

19
zärt - li - chen Trie - ben den Schön-sten, den Lieb-sten bald bei dir zu sehn, den
ten - der af - fec - tion, the pur - est, the fair - est, this day to re - ceive, the
25
Schön-sten! den Lieb - sten! Be - rei - te dich, Zi - on,
pur - est, the fair - est; pre - pare thy-self, Zi - on,
f
31
mit zärt - li - chen Trie - ben, be - rei - te dich,
with ten-der af - fec - tion, pre - pare thy - self,
tr
p
38
Zi - on, mit zärt - li - chen Trie - ben den Schön - sten, den Lieb - sten bald bei dir zu
Zi - on, with ten - der af - fec - tion, the pur - est, the fair - est this day to re -
tr

44
sehn, be - rei - te dich, Zi - on, mit zärt - li - chen Trie - ben den Schön-sten, den
ceive, pre - pare thy - self Zi - on, with ten - der af - fec - tion, the pur - est, the
tr
tr
50
Lieb-sten bald bei dir zu sehn, den Lieb-sten! den Schön - sten!
fair - est this day to re - ceive, the fair - est, the pur - est;
56
Be - rei - te dich, Zi - on, mit zärt - li - chen
pre - pare thy - self, Zi - on, with ten - der af -
f
tr
62
Trie-ben, be - rei - te dich, Zi - on, mit zärt - li - chen
fec - tion, pre - pare thy - self, Zi - on, with ten - der af -
p

68
Trie - ben _ den Schön - sten, den Lieb - sten bald bei dir _ zu _ sehn.
fec - tion, _ the pur - est, the fair - est this day to _ re - ceive.
tr
tr
f
75
tr
82
tr
[𝄐] *
[𝄐]
Fine
89
Dei - ne Wan - gen müs - sen heut _ viel schö - ner pran - gen,
Thou must meet Him with a heart _ with love _ o'er flow - ing,
p

*Fermatas on Fine (2nd time)

95
müs - sen heut viel schö - ner pran - gen, ei - le, den Bräu - ti - gam
with a heart with love o'er - flow - ing. Haste, then, with ar - dor the
101
sehn - lichst zu lie - ben, ei - le, ei - le, den Bräu - ti - gam
Bride-groom to wel - come, haste then haste then with ar - dor the
107
sehn - lichst zu lie - ben, ei - le, den Bräu - ti - gam
Bride - groom to wel - come, haste then with ar - dor the
113
sehn - lichst zu lie - ben.
Bride-groom to wel - come.
tr
f

120
Dei - ne Wan - gen müs - sen
Thou must meet Him with a
p
126
heut viel schö - ner pran - - - -
heart with love o'er - flow - - - -
132
- gen, ei - le, den Bräu-ti - gam sehn - lichst zu lie - ben.
- ing, haste then, with ar - dor the Bride - groom to wel-come.
tr
Da Capo al Fine

Schlafe, mein Liebster
(Slumber, beloved)
from
WEIHNACHTS – ORATORIUM
(Christmas Oratorio)

Johann Sebastian Bach

[Andante]
[p]
5
11
16

21

26
Schla - -
Slum - -
p

31
- fe, mein Lieb - - -
- ber, be - lov - - -

36
- ster, ge - nies - - se der Ruh,
- ed, and take thy re - pose,
41
schla - fe, mein Lieb - ster, ge - nies - se der Ruh, wa - che nach
Slum - ber, be - lov - ed, and take thy re - pose, soon wilt thou
46
die - sem vor al - ler Ge - dei - hen, schla - fe, mein Lieb - ster, ge -
wak - en, our joy and sal - va - tion. Slum - ber, be - lov - ed, and

51
nies - se der Ruh,
take thy re - pose,
wa - che nach die - sem vor al - ler Ge-dei -
soon wilt thou wak - en, our joy and sal-va -
56
hen!
tion.
f
61
66
Schla - fe, mein
Slum - ber; be -
p

70
Lieb - ster, ge - nies - se der Ruh, schla - fe, mein
lov - ed, and take thy re - pose, Slum - ber, be -
74
Lieb - ster, ge - nies - se der Ruh, wa - che nach
lov - ed and take thy re - pose. Soon wilt thou
78
die - sem vor al - ler Ge - dei - hen, wa - che nach
wa - ken, our joy and sal - va - tion, soon wilt thou

82
tr
die - sem vor al - ler Ge-dei - hen, wa - che, wa -
wak - en, our joy and sal-va - tion, wak - en, wak -
87
- che, wa - che nach die - sem, nach die - sem vor
- en, wak - en, O wak - en, soon wak - en our
92
tr
tr
al - - - - ler Ge-dei - hen!
joy and sal-va - tion.

97
f
102
107
112
La - be die Brust, emp - fin - de die
Oh, may thy breast find glad - ness and
*
p
Fine

*Fermata on Fine

116
Lust, wo wir un - ser Herz er - freu - - -
rest in our heart-felt ex - ul - ta - - -
120
- en, wo wir un - ser Herz er - freu - - -
- tion, in our heart-felt ex - ul - ta - - -
tr
124
- en, la - be die Brust, emp - fin - de die
- tion. Oh, may thy breast find glad - ness and

128
Lust, wo wir un - ser Herz er - freu - en, la -
rest in our heart-felt ex - ul - ta - tion, oh,
tr
132
- be die Brust, emp - fin - de die Lust, wo wir
may thy breast find glad - ness and rest, in our
tr
136
un - ser Herz er - freu - - - en, la -
heart-felt ex - ul - ta - - - tion, oh,
tr
tr
f

140
- be die Brust, emp - fin - de die Lust, wo wir
_ may thy breast find glad-ness and rest in our
p
f
p
144
un - ser _ Herz _ er - freu - - - -
heart-felt _ ex - ul - ta - - - - -
148
tr
D.C.
- - - - - - en!
- - - - - - tion.
tr

Schliesse, mein Herze
(Keep, O my spirit)
from
WEIHNACHTS – ORATORIUM
(Christmas Oratorio)

Johann Sebastian Bach

[Andante]
*
f

7

12

17

*Play small size notes in the absence of a violin.

21
25
Schlies - se, mein Her - ze, dies se - li - ge Wun - der fest
Keep, O my spir - it, this bless - ing and won - der close
p
30
in dei - nem Glau - ben ein, fest in dei - nem
with - in thy - self con - tain'd, close with - in thy -
35
Glau - ben ein! Schlies - se, mein Her - ze, dies se - li - ge
self con - tain'd. Keep, O my spir - it, this bless - ing and

40
Wun - der fest in dei-nem Glau - ben, in dei-nem Glau-ben ein!
won - der close with - in thy - self, close with - in thy - self con - tain'd.
45
Schlies - se, mein Her - ze, dies se - li - ge Wun - der fest in dei - nem
Keep, O my spir - it, this bless - ing and won - der close with - in thy -
50
Glau - ben ein, fest in dei-nem Glau - ben, fest
self con - tain'd, close with - in thy - self con-tain'd, close
55
in dei - nem Glau - ben, in dei - nem Glau-ben ein, fest in dei - nem
with - in thy - self con-tain'd, with - in thy - self con - tain'd, close with - in thy -

60
Glau - ben ein!
self con - tain'd.
f
65
71
Las - se dies Wun - der der gött - li - chen
O! by the won - ders thy Sav - iour hath
tr
p
76
Wer - ke im - mer zur Stär - ke dei - nes schwa - chen
shew'd thee, of His great mer - cy, be thy fee - ble

81
Glau - bens sein! Las - se dies Wun - der der gött - li - chen
faith sus - tain'd! O! by the won - ders thy Sav - iour hath
86
Wer - ke im - mer zur Stär - ke dei - nes schwa - chen Glau - bens
shew'd thee, of His great mer - cy, be thy fee - ble faith sus -
92
sein, im - mer zur Stär - ke dei - nes schwa - chen
tain'd! O! by His won - ders be thy fee - ble
97
Glau - bens sein!
faith sus - tain'd!
tr
f

103
Schlies - se, mein Her - ze, dies se - li-ge Wun - der fest in dei-nem
Keep, O my spir - it, this bless - ing and won - der close with - in thy -
p
108
Glau - ben, in dei - nem Glau-ben ein, fest in dei-nem Glau - ben, in
self, close with - in thy - self con - tain'd, close with - in thy - self, close with-
113
dei - nem Glau-ben ein! Schlies - se, mein Her - ze, dies se - li-ge
in thy - self con - tain'd. Keep, O my spir - it, this bless - ing and
118
Wun - der fest in dei-nem Glau-ben ein, fest in dei-nem Glau -
won - der close with - in thy - self con-tain'd, close with-in thy - self,

124
- ben, in dei-nem Glau-ben ein, fest in dei-nem Glau -
close with-in thy - self con - tain'd, close with-in thy - self
tr
130
- ben ein, fest in dei - nem Glau - ben ein!
con - tain'd, close with - in thy - self con - tain'd.
tr
f
136
142

Schliesse, mein Herze
(Keep, O my spirit)
from
WEIHNACHTS – ORATORIUM
(Christmas Oratorio)

Johann Sebastian Bach

[Andante]
Violin
[f]
6
13
19
24
[p]
30
37
42

The part may be carefully cut from the book.

48
54
61
[f]
68
tr
73
79
85
91

97
[f]
[p]
104
110
116
121
126
tr
131
[f]
137
142

Inflammatus et accensus
from
STABAT MATER

Antonín Dvořák

Andante maestoso (♩ = 54)
f
marcato

4
In - flam-ma - tus
dim.
p
sim.

7
et ___ ac-cen - sus Per te, Vir - go, sim de - fen - sus In
pp

10
di - e ju - di - ci - i, In-flam - ma - tus et ac-
13
cen - sus Per te, Vir-go, sim de-fen-sus In di - e ju -
pp
16
di - ci - i.
f
f marcato
19
p
dim.

21
p
In - flam-ma - tus et ac - cen - sus
pp
25
p
Per te, Vir - go, sim de - fen - sus In di - e ju -
p
28
di - ci - i,
pp
In - flam - ma - tus et ac - cen - sus

31
Per te, Vir - go, sim de - fen - sus In di - e ju -
pp
35
pp
di - ci - i.
f
Fac me cru - ce
pp
p
f
39
cus - to - di - ri, Mor - te Chris - ti præ - mu - ni - ri,
p

42
rit.
Con - fo - ve - ri gra - - - ti -
pp
rit.
45
a tempo
pp
a, con - fo - ve - ri, con - fo - ve - ri
a tempo
pp
48
gra - ti - a.
f

51

p

Fac ___ me cru - ce cus - to-di - ri, ___ Mor - te Chris - ti ___

p

54

f

præ - mu-ni - ri, Con - fo-ve - ri, con - fo-ve - ri,

p

57

con - fo-ve - ri gra - ti - a.

pp

60
p
Fac me cru - ce cus - to - di - ri,
pp
63
dim.
Mor - te Chris - ti præ - - - mu - ni - ri,
65
p
Con - fo - ve - ri, con - fo - ve - ri
f
pp
Ped.

67
f
gra - ti - a, con - fo - ve - ri gra - ti - a,
70
f
con - fo - ver - ri gra - ti-
dim.
pp
73
f
a. Fac me cru - ce cus - to - di - ri,
pp
p

76
p
Mor - te Chris - ti præ - mu - ni - ri, Con - fo - ver - ri, con - fo - ve - ri,
p
79
f rit.
con - fo - ve - ri gra - - - ti -
f rit.
dim
81
a tempo
a.
p a tempo
ten.
pp

Virgam virtutis
from
DIXIT DOMINUS

George Frideric Handel

[Andante]
mf
3
5
7
Vir - gam vir - tu - tis, ___ vir - tu - tis tu - ae,
p
mf

10
vir-gam vir - tu - tis, virtu-tis tu - ae e - mit - tet
p
13
Do - mi-nus, e - mit - tet Do - mi-nus ex Si -
tr
tr
15
on, e - mit - tet Do - - - - -
17
- - - - mi-nus ex Si -

19
on: do - mi - na - - -
21
- - - - - - - -
23
- - - - - - - - -
25
- re in me - - - - -

27
- - di-o i - ni - mi - co -
29
[tr]
- rum tu - o - rum, i - ni - mi -
31
tr
- co - rum tu - o - rum, do -
33
- - mi-na - re, do - mi-na - re in me -

35
tr
- di - o ___ in - ni - mi - co - rum tu - o - rum,
37
do - mi - na - re, do - mi - na - re
39
in me - di - o i - ni - mi - co - rum tu -
41
o - rum, i - ni - mi - co - - - -

43
tr
rum tu - o - rum, i - ni - mi - co -
46
tr
rum tu - o - rum.
49
51

Father of Heav'n!

from

JUDAS MACCABÆUS

George Frideric Handel

Andante larghetto
p
3
5
7
PRIEST:
Fa - ther of Heav'n!

10
Fa - ther of Heav'n! from Thy e - ter - nal throne, from
12
Thy e - ter - nal throne look with an eye of
14
bless - ing down, while we pre - pare,
16
with ho - ly rites, to sol - em - nize the Feast of

18
Lights.
Fa -
f
p
20
- - ther of Heav'n! from Thy e - ter - nal ___ throne
f
22
look with an ___ eye of ___ bless - ing ___ down,
p
24
while we pre - pare, ___

26
with ho - ly rites, to sol - em - nize,
28
the Feast of Lights, the Feast of Lights, to
30
sol - em - nize the Feast of Lights, while we pre - pare, with
33
ho - ly rites, to sol - em - nize the Feast of Lights,

36
38
and thus our grate - ful hearts em -
p
40
ploy,
and in Thy praise
this al - tar raise
43
with car - ols of tri-umph-ant
joy,
this al - tar
raise with car - ols of tri-umph-ant
f

46
joy,
with car-ols of tri - umph - ant joy.
3
49
ad lib.
Fa - ther of Heav'n!
from
f
p
53
Thy e - ter - nal throne,
from Thy e - ter - nal throne
55
look with an eye of bless - ing down,
while we pre -

57
pare, with ho - ly rites, to
59
sol - em - nize the Feast of Lights, the Feast of
61
Lights, to sol - em - nize the
3
63
Feast of Lights.
f

O thou that tellest good tidings to Zion

from

MESSIAH

George Frideric Handel

Recit.
Be - hold! a vir - gin shall con-ceive, and bear a son,
4
and shall call his name Em - man - u - el: God with us.
Aria
Andante
f
tr
4

7
10
tr
tr
tr
O
p
13
thou that tell - est good ti - dings to Zi - on,
[f]
16
get thee up in - to the high moun - tain!
[p]
[f]

19
O thou that tell - est good
[p]
22
ti - dings to Zi - on,
get thee
[f]
[p]
25
up in - to the high moun - - - -
28
- tain!
Get thee up in - to the high

31

moun - - - - - - -

35

- tain!

tr

f

38

O

tr

[*p*]

41

thou that tell - est good ti - dings _ to Je - ru - sa - lem, lift

f

p

44
up thy voice with strength! Lift it
47
up, be not a - fraid! Say un - to the
50
cit - ies of Ju - dah, say un - to the cit - ies of Ju - dah,
53
Be - hold your God! Be - hold your God! Say

58
un - to the cit - ies of Ju - dah, be -
61
hold your God! Be - hold your God!
65
Be - hold your God!
f
69
O
[p]

72
thou that tell - est good ti - dings to Zi - on,
[f]
75
a - rise, shine, for thy light is come;
[p]
78
a - rise, a -
[p]
81
rise, a - rise, shine, for thy light is come,

84
and the glo - - - -
87
- ry of the Lord, the
90
glo - ry of ___ the Lord ___ is
p
93
ris - en, ___ is ris - en ___ up - on ___ thee, _ is ris - en, is

97
ris - en up - on thee, the glo - ry, the
100
glo - ry, the glo - ry of the Lord
103
is ris - en up - on thee.

He was despised
from
MESSIAH

George Frideric Handel

Largo
He was de - spis - ed,
de - spis - ed __ and re - ject - ed, re -

13
ject - ed of men;
a man of sor - rows,
pp
16
a man of sor - rows, and ac - quaint - ed with grief,
19
a man of sor - rows, and ac - quaint - ed with grief.
pp
p
tr
22
He
tr
f
f
p

25

was de - spis - ed, re - ject - ed, He was de -

28

spis - ed and re - ject - ed of men; a man ___ of sor - rows, and ac - quaint - ed with

31

grief, ___ a man of sor - rows, and ac - quaint - ed with grief.

34

He was de - spis - ed, re - ject - ed; a man _ of ___

tr *tr*

p

37
[tr]
sor - rows, and ac - quaint - ed with grief, and ac - quaint - ed with grief,
tr
40
[ad lib. on D.C.]
a man of sor - rows, and ac - quaint - ed with grief.
tr
f
44
tr
tr
tr
tr
48
Fine
He gave His back to the
un poco piano

51
smit - ers,
He gave His back to the
53
smit - ers,
and His cheeks to
them that pluck - ed off the
55
hair, and His cheeks to
them that pluck - ed off the
57
hair, and his cheeks to
them that pluck - ed off the

59
hair: He hid not His face from shame and
61
spit - ting, He hid not His face from shame,
63
from shame, He hid not His
65
opt.
D.C. al Fine
face from shame, from shame and spit-ting.

But who may abide
from
MESSIAH

George Frideric Handel

Larghetto
mf

7
But who may a -
[p]

14
bide the day of His com - ing? And who shall_ stand when
[f]
[p]

21
He ap - pear - eth? Who shall stand when
[f]
[p]
27
He ap - pear - eth? But who may a - bide, but
[f]
[p]
33
who may a - bide the day of His com - ing? And
[f]
[p]
39
who shall stand when He ap - pear - eth?

44
And who shall stand when
49
He ap - pear - - - -
54
- eth? When He ap - pear -
(tr)
59
Prestissimo
eth?
[mf]

61
63
For He is like a re-
65
fin - er's fire,
67
for He is like a re-

69
fin - - - - - - - -
71
- - - er's fire.
73
Who shall stand when He ap -
75
pear - eth? For He is like a re -

77
fin
81
er's fire, for
85
He is like a re - fin
87
er's fire,

90
tr
and who shall stand when He ap - pear - eth?
p
f
p
f
94
Larghetto (Tempo I)
But who may a - bide the day of His com-ing?
[p]
f
101
And who shall stand, and who shall stand when He ap -
[p]
108
[ad lib.]
pear - eth?
When He ap - pear - eth?

115
Prestissimo
For He is like a re - fin - er's
118
fire, like a re - fin - er's
120
fire, and who shall stand when He,
123
when He ap - pear - eth? And who shall

126
stand
when
He
ap -
p
128
pear - eth?
For
He
is
130
like
a re - fin - er's
132
fire,
and
who
shall

134
stand
when
He
ap
-
136
pear
-
eth,
when
He
ap
-
138
pear
-
eth?
For
He
is
140
like
a
re
-
fin
-
-
-
p

143
tr
tr
146
Adagio
[ad lib. cadenza]
er's fire,
for He is like a re - fin - er's
151
Prestissimo
fire.
f
153
155

Thou art gone up on high

from

MESSIAH

George Frideric Handel

Allegro larghetto
f
6
11
Thou art gone up on high, thou art gone up on high,
p
f
f
17
thou hast led cap-ti - vi-ty cap - tive, thou hast led cap-ti - vi-ty cap - tive, and re -

22
cei - - - ved gifts for men; yea, e - ven
p
29
for thine en - - - - e-mies, yea,
35
e - ven for thine en - e - mies,
f
41
that the Lord God might dwell a - mong them, that the Lord
[p]

47
God might dwell
53
[tr]
a - mong them, might dwell a - mong them.
f
59
Thou art gone up on high, thou art gone up on high, thou hast
p
65
led cap-ti - vi-ty cap - tive, thou hast led cap-ti - vi-ty cap - tive, and re -

70
cei - ved, and re - cei - ved gifts for men, and re -
[p]
76
cei - ved gifts for thine en - e - mies, that the Lord God might dwell a -
82
mong _ them, and might dwell
88
a - mong _ them, that the Lord _ God might

94
dwell a - mong them,
100
[tr]
that the Lord, the Lord God might dwell a - mong them.
f
106
112

Fac me vere tecum flere
from
STABAT MATER

Franz Joseph Haydn

Lachrymoso
p sempre legato
f
p
tr
f
f
tr
Fac
me
p

11
ve - re te - cum fle - re, te - cum fle - re
f
13
cru - ci - fi - xo con - do - le - re, do-nec
p
15
e - go, do-nec e - go vi - xe - ro. Fac me
17
ve - re te-cum fle - re cru-ci - fi - xo con - do - le - re, con-do -

19
le - re, do-nec e - go, do-nec e - go, do-nec e - go
tr
21
vi - xe - ro, do-nec e - go, do-nec e -
23
tr
- - go vi - xe - ro.
f
f
25
tr

27
Jux - ta cru - cem te - cum, te - cum sta - re,
p
3
29
et me ti - bi so - ci - a - re in planc - tu de -
31
si - de - ro, in planc - tu de - si - de - ro. Jux - ta
33
cru - cem te - cum sta - re, et me ti - bi so - ci - a - re in

35
planc - tu de - si - de - ro, in planc - -
37
- - tu de - si - de - ro, et me
39
ti - bi so - ci - a - re in planc - tu de - si - de -
tr
41
ro, in planc - tu, in planc - - tu, in
*

*Though in the orchestra, this section is optional in the piano reduction.

43
planc - tu, in planc - tu de - si - de -
tr
f
45
ro.
f
p
47
tr
f
p
49
f
tr

O rest in the Lord
(Sei stille dem Herrn)
from
ELIJAH

Andantino ♩ = 72
Felix Mendelssohn
THE ANGEL p
O rest in the Lord, wait pa-tient-ly for Him, and He shall
Sei stil-le dem Herrn, und war-te auf ihn; der wird dir
pp
4
give thee thy heart's de-sires: O rest in the Lord, wait pa-tient-ly for
ge-ben was dein Herz wünscht; sei stil-le dem Herrn, und war-te auf
7
Him, and He shall give thee thy heart's de-sires, and He shall
ihn; der wird dir ge-ben was dein Herz wünscht; der wird dir

10
give thee thy heart's de - sires. Com-mit thy way un - to Him, and trust in
ge - ben was dein Herz wünscht. Be - fiehl ihm dei - ne We - ge und hof - fe auf
[p]
13
Him; com - mit thy way un - to Him, and trust in
ihn; be - fiehl ihm dei - ne We - ge und hof - fe auf
15
Him, and fret not thy - self be - cause of e - vil -
ihn. Steh' ab vom Zorn, und lass den

17
p
do - ers. O rest in the Lord, wait pa - tient - ly for Him, wait pa - tient - ly for
Grimm. Sei stil - le dem Herrn und war - te auf ihn, war - te auf
p
pp
20
Him; O rest in the Lord, wait pa - tient - ly for Him, and He shall
ihn! Sei stil - le dem Herrn und war - te auf ihn; der wird dir
23
give thee thy heart's de - sires, and He shall give thee thy heart's de -
ge - ben was dein Herz wünscht, der wird dir ge - ben was dein Herz
cresc.
sf
p

26
sires, and He shall give thee thy heart's de -
wünscht, der wird dir ge - ben was dein Herz
sf
p
28
p
cresc.
sires. O rest in the Lord, O rest in the Lord, and wait,
wünscht. Sei stil - le dem Herrn, sei stil - le dem Herrn, und war -
cresc.
31
p
wait pa - tient - ly for Him.
- te, und war - te auf ihn.
tr
pp

Woe unto them who forsake Him

(Weh ihnen, dass sie von mir weichen)

from

ELIJAH

Felix Mendelssohn

Lento (♪ = 96)
Woe, woe un - to them who for - sake Him! de - struc - tion shall fall up -
Weh ih - nen, dass sie von mir wei - chen! sie müs - sen ver - stö - ret
p
5
on them: for they have trans - gress - ed, trans - gress - ed a - gainst Him. Though
wer - den, denn sie sind ab - trün - nig von mir ge - wor - den. Ich
p
10
they are by Him re - deem - ed, by Him re - deem - ed, though they are by Him re -
woll - te sie wohl er - lö - sen, sie wohl er - lö - sen, ich woll - te sie wohl er -
p

15
cresc.
deem - ed, yet they have spo - ken false - ly a - gainst Him, spo - ken
lö - sen, wenn sie nicht Lü - gen wi - der mich lehr - ten, wenn sie nicht
cresc.
19
f
p
false - ly a - gainst Him. Woe, woe un - to them who for - sake Him! de -
Lü - gen lehr - ten; Weh ih - nen, dass sie von mir wei - chen, sie
f
dim.
pp
24
cresc.
sf
struc - tion shall fall up - on them. Though they are by Him re -
müs - sen ver - stö - ret wer - den. Ich woll - te sie wohl er -
cresc.
pp

27
cresc.
f
opt.
deem - ed; from Him have they fled; though they are by Him re - deem - ed;
lö - sen; sie hö - ren es nicht. Ich woll - te sie wohl er - lö - sen,
cresc.
cresc.
32
p
e - ven from Him they have fled. Woe un - to them!
a - ber sie hö - ren es nicht. Weh ih - nen!
pp
37
Woe un - to them!
Weh ih - nen!
pp

Laudamus te
from
MASS IN C MINOR

Wolfgang Amadeus Mozart

Allegro aperto
p
f

5
p
tr
f

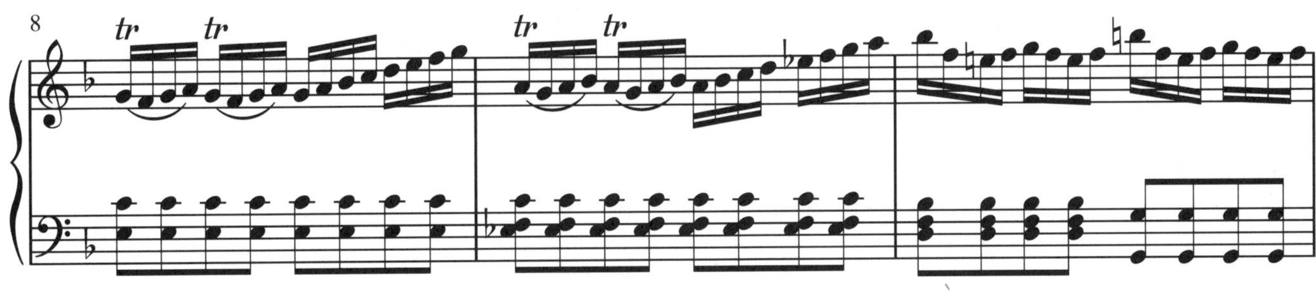
8
tr

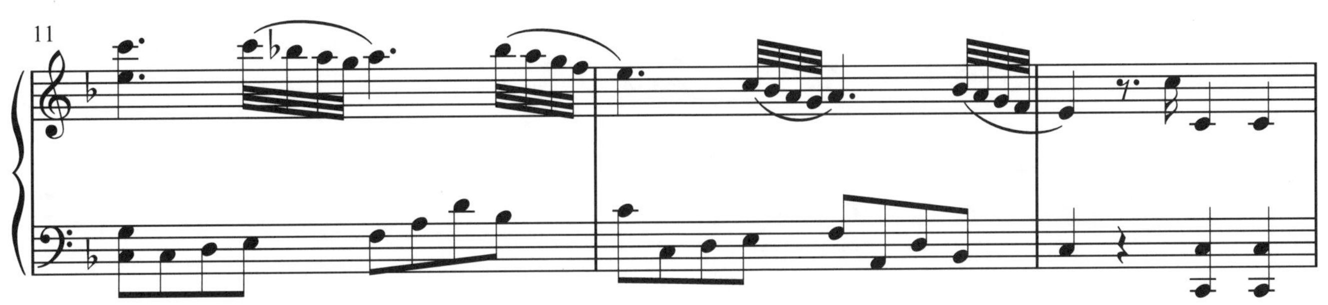
11

14
Lau - da - mus - te,
p
f
19
be - ne - di - ci - mus - te,
be - ne -
p
f
p
24
di - ci - mus - te,
tr
27
a - do - ra - mus te,
glo - ri - fi - ca - mus te
tr

31
glo - ri - fi - ca
35
39
43
mus _ te.

46
Ad - o - ra - mus _ te.
fp
fp
49
Glo - ri - fi -
fp
fp
52
ca - - - - - - -
tr♭
tr
56

59
tr
- - - - mus te.
cresc.
tr tr
f
62
tr tr
tr tr
65
Lau - da - mus te, a-do-
fp
p
sim.
69
ra - mus te. Be - ne - di - ci-mus
fp

73
te, glo - ri - fi - ca - mus - te, glo - ri - fi - ca - mus - te,
fp
fp
78
lau - da - mus te, a - do - ra - mus te.
fp
fp
fp
mfp
f
82
Lau - da -
tr
tr
tr
p
87
- - - - - mus te,
f

91
be - ne - di - ci - mus te,
p
f
95
be - ne - di - ci - mus te,
p
tr
99
a - do - ra - mus te,
102
glo - ri - fi - ca - - - - -

106
109
tr
tr
113
tr
tr
mus
117
te.
A
do
fp
fp

120
ra - mus _ te.
123
Glo - ri - fi - ca - - - -
fp
fp
tr
tr
127
130
mus te, glo -
fp

133
ri - fi - ca - - - -
fp
fp
136
tr
- - - - mus te.
p
cresc.
tr tr
f
139
tr tr
tr tr
141

Quæ mœrebat et dolebat
from
STABAT MATER

Giovanni Battista Pergolesi

Allegro
f

6
p
tr

11
f
p

16
f

21
Quæ mœ -
p
26
re - bat et do - le - bat, et do - le - bat,
31
tr
tr
et tre - me - bat, dum vi - de - bat na - ti
36
pœ - nas, pœ - nas in - cly - ti, et tre - me - bat,

41
dum vi - de-bat na - ti pœ - nas, na - ti pœ - nas
p
f
47
in - cly - ti, et tre - me-bat, cum vi -
p
52
de-bat na - ti pœ - nas, na - ti pœ - nas in - cly -
p
f
58
ti. Quæ mœ -
tr tr
f
p

64
tr tr
re - bat et do - le - bat, et do - le - bat,
f
69
tr tr tr tr
et tre - me - bat, dum vi - de - bat,
74
dum vi - de - bat, et tre -
f
p
79
tr
me - bat, dum vi - de - bat na - ti pœ - nas,

84
tr
tr
na - ti pœ - nas in - cly - ti, et tre -
f
p
89
me - bat, dum vi - de - bat na - ti pœ - nas,
94
tr
tr
na - ti pœ - nas in - cly - ti.
f
f
99
p
f

Eija, mater, fons amoris
from
STABAT MATER

Giovanni Battista Pergolesi

[Allegro]
f
p
f
p
f
E - ija, ma - ter, fons a - mo - ris,
p
fons a - mo - ris, me sen - ti - re vim do -
3
f

23
lo - ris, vim do - lo - ris; fac, ut te - cum
29
lu - ge - am, lu - ge - am.
35
40
E - ija, ma - ter, fons a - mo - ris, fons a - mo - ris,

46
me — sen - ti - re vim — do - lo - ris; fac, ut
p
p
52
te - cum lu - ge - am, fac, ut
58
te - cum lu - ge - am. E - ija, ma - ter, fons — a -
f
p
65
mo - ris, me — sen - ti - re vim — do - lo - ris, vim

71
Largo
do - lo - ris; fac, ut te - cum
f
p
77
lu - ge - am, fac, ut te - cum lu - ge -
f
p
83
am, lu - ge - am.
f
p
89
f
p
f
p

Fac ut portem
from
STABAT MATER

Giovanni Battista Pergolesi

Largo

Fac ut por - tem Chri - sti mor - tem,

9
Chri - sti mor - tem, pas - sio - nis fac con - sor - tem, et
fp
11
pla - - - - - - gas
13
re - co - le-re.
f
16
Fac me pla - gis vul - ne - ra - ri,
p

18

vul - ne - ra - ri, cru-ce hac in - e - bri - a - ri, in -

20

e - bri - a - ri, ob a - mo -

22

- - rem fi - lii, ob a - mo - rem fi - li - i, ob a -

p

24 **Largo** [*a tempo*]

mo - rem fi - li - i.

Vouchsafe, O Lord
from
TE DEUM LAUDAMUS

Henry Purcell

[Largo]
Vouch - safe,
O
Lord,
to
keep us this day with -
out
sin.
O Lord,
O Lord,
have mer - cy,
have mer - cy,
have
p
[cresc.]

15
mer - cy up - on us,
have mer - cy,
mer - - - cy up - on us.
O
Lord,
O
Lord,
let Thy mer - cy,
let Thy
18
22
26
[f]
[p]
[cresc.]

30
mer - cy light - - - - - en up -
34
on us, as our trust
f
38
is in Thee, as our trust
p
42
is in Thee.

Agnus Dei
from
MESSE SOLENNELLE

Gioachino Rossini

Andante sostenuto (♪ = 88)
ppp

4
p
ff
mf
ff
f
ff
sf

8
ppp

9

10
dolce
A - gnus
11
3
De - i qui tol - lis pec - ca - ta
12
f
mun - di qui tol - lis pec - ca - ta
f
13
pp
mun - di mi - se -
pp

14
re - re mi - se - re - re
15
3
no - bis qui tol - lis pec -
16
f
- ca - ta pec - ca - ta
f
17
pp
mun - di mi - se - re - re
pp

18
mi - se - re - re no -
19
bis.
pp
21
ppp
22
dolce
A - gnus

23
3
De - i qui tol - lis pec - ca - ta
24
f
mun - di qui tol - lis pec - ca - ta
f
25
pp
mun - di mi - se -
ppp
26
re - re mi - se - re - re

27
3
no - bis qui tol - lis pec -
28
ff
f
- ca - ta pec - ca - ta
29
pp
ppp
mun - di mi - se - re - re
30
mi - se - re - re no -

31
bis.
pp
33
ppp
34
dolce
A - gnus
35
3
De - i qui tol - lis pec - ca - ta

36
f
mun - di qui tol - lis pec - ca - ta
f
37
pp
mun - di do - na
pp
38
no - bis pa - - -
39
cem
do - na

40
no - bis pa - - -
sim.
41
cem do - - na
42
f
no - - bis do - - na
f
43
no - bis do - na
pp

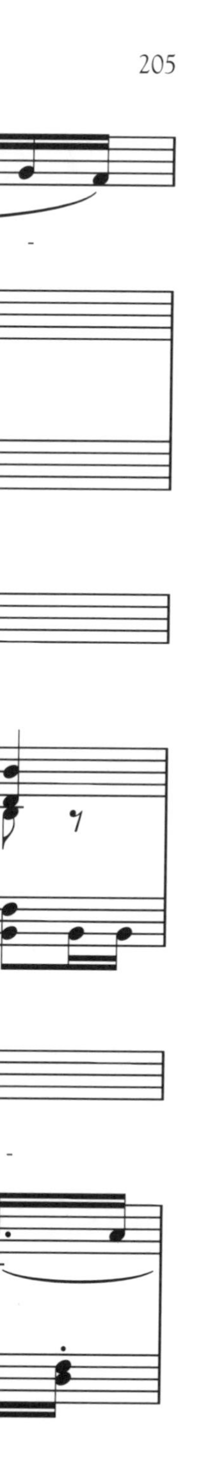
44
do - na no - bis pa -
pp
45
cem.
47
p
Qui tol -
ppp
48
lis pec - ca -

49
cresc.
ta
pec - ca - ta
cresc.
50
rinforz.
mun - di
mi - se - re - re
mi - se -
rinforz.
51
f
re - re
mi - se - re - re
f
52
ff
no - bis
do - na
no - bis
pa -
ff

53
ppp
cem
qui
tol
ppp
54
lis
pec
ca
55
cresc.
ta
pec
ca
ta
cresc.
56
rinforz.
mun
di
mi
se
re
re
mi
se
rinforz.

57
f
re - re mi - se - re - re
f
58
tutta forza
ff
no - - bis do - - na
ff tutta forza
59
no - bis pa - - -

60
cem.
tutta forza
61
62
ppp
p
66
ff
mf
ff
f
ff
fff

Fac ut portem
from
STABAT MATER

Gioachino Rossini

Andante grazioso (♪ = 104)
dolce
4
dolce
7
ff
p
10
ff
13
pp
Fac ut por - tem Chris - ti mor - tem, pas - si -

16
o - nis _ e - jus sor - tem et pla - gas re - co - le - re,
20
et
pla - gas
f
p
23
f
re - - - - co - le - re.
ff
pp
27
ff
pp
ff
pp

29

Fac me pla - gis vul - ne -

ff *p*

31

ra - ri,

ff *pp* *ff* *pp*

33

cru - ce hac i - ne - bri -

ff *p*

35

a - ri, ob a - mo - rem fi - li -

37
i, ob a - mo - rem fi - li -
39
i, ob a - mo - rem fi - li - i: fac me pla-gis vul-ne -
p
ff
pp
43
ra - ri, cru - ce hac i - ne - bri - a - ri, ob a - mo - rem fi - li -
47
i, ob
f
p

a - mo - rem fi - li -
i, ob a - mo - rem
fi - li - i.

Liber scriptus
from
MESSA DI REQUIEM

Giuseppe Verdi

[Molto meno mosso]
pp
con 8va sotto
con 8va sotto
5
con 8va sotto
con 8va sotto
con 8va sotto
(loco)
ppp
10
Allegro molto sostenuto (♩ = 88)
dim.
pp
Li - ber scri - ptus pro - fe - re - tur,
p
pp
6
ppp
14
dim.
pp
In quo to - tum con - ti - ne - tur,
6
ppp

18
Un - de mun - dus, Un - de
mf
f
20
mun - dus ju - di - ce - tur, Un - de
f
22
mun - dus, Un - de mun - dus ju - di - ce -
p
col canto
25
tur.
p
f

30
ff
Ju - dex er - go cum se -
ff
pp
de - bit, Quid -
cresc.
6
36
pp
- quid la - tet ap - pa - re - bit, Nil i -
dolce
p
41
poco accelerando
nul - tum re - ma - ne - bit, Quid-quid la - tet ap - pa - re - bit, Nil i -

46
a tempo
mf
nul - tum, Nil i - nul - tum
mf a tempo
6 6 6 6
48
re - ma - ne - bit, re - ma -
6 6 6 6 6 6 6 6
50
ne - bit, Nil i - nul - tum Nil i - nul - tum re - ma-
f f
6 6 6 6
p
3
53
un poco
ne - bit. Li - ber
6 6
p

55
scri - ptus pro - fe - re - tur, In quo
cresc.
57
to - tum con - ti - ne - tur, Un - de
cresc. sempre
59
mun - - dus ju - - di -
60
ff
ce - - - - tur. Ju - dex
ff
pp
ppp

63
ppp
er - go cum se - de - bit, Quid - quid la - tet ap - pa - re - bit, Nil
ancora più p
68
sempre più p
morendo
i - nul-tum re-ma-ne-bit, Nil, Nil,
72
ff
Nil! Li - ber scri-ptus pro - fe - re - tur.
perdendosi
vuota
ff
p col canto

Qui sedes ad dexteram Patris
from
GLORIA

Antonio Vivaldi

Allegro
[f]
8
14
tr
20
27
Qui se - - des ad dex -

34

- te - ram Pa - tris, mi - se - re -

41

- - - - - - -

48

- - re, mi - se - re - re, mi - se -

56

tr

re - re ______ no - bis.

[*f*]

63
Qui se - des ad dex - te - ram Pa - tris,
70
mi - se - re - - - -
76
- - - re no - bis,
tr
82
mi - se - re - -

89
tr
- re no - bis.
96
Qui se - des ad dex -
104
- te - ram Pa - tris, mi - se - re - - -
111
- - re, mi - se - re - re,

118
tr
mi - se - re - re ______ no - bis, mi - se -
125
re - re, mi - se - re - re, mi - se - re - re ____ no - bis.
132
138
144
tr

Esurientes implevit
from
MAGNIFICAT

Antonio Vivaldi

Allegro
f
4
7
E-su - ri - en-tes im-ple - vit_ bo-nis et di - vi-tes di -
p
10
tr
mi-sit, di - mi - sit i - na-nes, in-a - - -

13
tr
tr
- nes, et di - vi - tes di - mi - sit, di - mi-sit in-a - nes.
f
16
E - su - ri - en - tes im - ple - vit bo - nis,
p
19
e - su - ri - en - tes im - ple - vit bo - nis, et di - vi - tes di - mi - sit, et
22
di - vi - tes di - mi - sit, di - mi - sit in - a - nes, et di-vi - tes di - mi - sit in -
p

25
a - - - - - - -
27
- - nes, et di-vi-tes di - mi - sit in - a - nes, et
30
di - vi - tes_di - mi - sit, di - mi - sit_in - a - nes, in -
32
a - nes, in-a - nes.
f